Introduction

Easy to Make! Easy to Read!

Children will love creating their own versions of favorite Bible stories, special prayers, and songs of praise found in the Old Testament. The books in the *Make Your Own Bible Stories* series provide children with interactive, personalized reading experiences by inviting them to investigate, complete sentence frames, illustrate, assemble, and create covers for their very own readers. This book contains 10 eight-page, themed, reproducible Little Books for emergent readers. These easy-to-read Little Books contain text that is simple, repetitive, and reader-friendly. Each Little Book contains a well-loved story from the Old Testament along with direct Bible quotes and other Christian values and principles.

This book provides everything you need to get children excited about reading and God's love for us as they create their very own library of self-made and illustrated Old Testament Bible stories.

This book includes:

Creative Suggestions and Activities

Pages 3–7 provide creative suggestions and activities for each Little Book, including these three aspects:

Cover Idea—This gives directions on how to create a colorful, eye-catching cover using a variety of art techniques and mediums.

Ideas for Illustrating Inside Pages—These help you guide the children to add their own text to many of the books and to creatively illustrate the pages.

Extension Activities—These provide unique ways to extend learning concepts presented in the Little Books as well as encourage further reading and writing.

Literature List

A comprehensive list of children's Bibles, Bible stories, and related books is provided on page 8. Use these books as read-alouds, research material, and extra books children can read on their own. Read-alouds can enhance your religious education program by providing background knowledge and extending the spiritual concepts introduced in the Little Books.

Directions for Making the Little Books

Putting the Pages Together

Reproduce the pages for each Little Book. *Do not cut pages in half!* Children can fold the pages and place them in numerical order. The pages will be doubled, and text will read on both sides. This unique page construction creates more durable books for frequent rereading. Also, creating artwork is easier. Markers and paint will not bleed through, and the pages are more suitable for decorative materials.

Note: Depending on the art technique used, it may be easier for children to illustrate each page before assembling the books, especially if it's a messy technique! Have extra pages available for "mess-ups." Once the art is complete and pages are in order, fold the pages on the dotted lines and bind them together. Stapling is the easiest, but pages can also be hole-punched and bound with ribbon or yarn.

Adding a Cover and Completing the Pages

- The first page of each Little Book can serve as the cover. However, you may choose to follow the cover suggestions on pages 3–7, or you can invite each child to make a special, individualized cover of his or her own. Make two covers at a time by cutting 12" x 18" (30 cm x 45 cm) sheets of construction paper in half lengthwise and then folding each piece in half.
- The inside pages can be illustrated quickly and easily by drawing and/or coloring. (Refer to the Literature List on page 8 for books that help children learn to draw.) Or, you may follow the suggestions on pages 3–7 for more visually-exciting art. In many instances, children are asked to complete existing art and/or draw inside borders or frames. These suggestions are a great way to integrate the arts into your program, and children will love experimenting with pastels, paint, crayon-resist, cut paper, and more!
- In advance, make several photocopies of your class picture. Children can use their own pictures whenever a self-portrait or photo is called for in the art. Or, you can use photocopied pictures to create a "Meet the Author" page for special books.
- You may also attach a "comments" page on the inside back covers of the books. Here, children can dictate or write their feelings about the book, what they learned, or more text additions to continue the story.
- To encourage rereading, attach a page to the inside back covers on which children can list the people to whom they have read their books.

Using the Little Books

Before children make and read the Little Books on their own, expose the children to the complete Bible stories featured or the related scriptures several times. You may choose to read the stories from a children's Bible or engage them more fully by telling the story with visual aids such as picture posters, feltboard pieces, or with a film strip or video. Learning a related song also helps to create enthusiasm as well as set the stage. Next, introduce the exact text in the Little Books through shared reading activities. Depending on the children's reading skill development, they should have several opportunities to interact with the text before making each Little Book. You can do this in a variety of ways:

- Make a class big book using the text from the Little Book combined with the children's illustrations. Read the big book together several times.
- Make a pocket chart of the Little Book's text, along with matching picture cards.
- Make overhead transparencies of the Little Book's text and art.

Just think how proud children will be showing off their own creatively-designed books to their classmates and families! There are a myriad of ways to use these books in your classroom and at home, but below are just a few suggestions on how to incorporate the Little Books into your program. Use them as . . .

- Learning center activities
- Special activities for holidays and special days
- Independent reading material
- Homework activities
- Bible stories and books of prayer the children can take home

Creative Suggestions and Activities

God Made the World

Cover Idea

Cut a circle from tagboard. Paint it with a swirly pattern using blue and brown tempera paints to create a planet earth. When dry, glue the earth to a black construction paper cover. Write the book's title with yellow puffy paint or white crayon. Use construction paper scraps to create stars and a moon to complete the cover design.

Inside Pages

Outline the designs on each page with thick lines of black crayon. Paint within the black lines using watercolor paints. Use black and yellow watercolors to represent dark and light on page 2. Add details to each page using stickers, drawings, fabric scraps, or other decorative items. For example, add trees, flowers, and other plants to page 4; sun, moon, and stars to page 5; fish and birds to page 6; animals and people to page 7.

Extension Activities

- Divide the children into small groups and assign each group one page of text from the poem. Each group uses tagboard and other art supplies to create simple props depicting the text it was assigned. Then let the children perform the story of Creation by having each group recite its verse while displaying its props. Begin by darkening the room. Have a volunteer turn on the lights for the first verse, *"Let there be light!"* The children can perform the story for other children or parents.
- Create a big book version of the story using the artwork the children designed from the activity described above. Glue their "props" to large book pages cut from butcher paper. Add text and let the children enhance the art using tempera paint, markers, crayons, and other art supplies.

Who Built the Ark?

Cover Idea

Use brown construction paper to make an ark-shaped cover for the book. Add details using markers. Add a few pairs of animal stickers to the ark or make animals from construction paper scraps.

Inside Pages

Glue thin pieces of tree bark or wood scraps to page 3. Finish the artwork on page 4 by drawing scenery, Noah, his family, or perhaps some animals. Draw and color pairs of animals on pages 5 through 7. On page 8, draw and color pairs of animals and write their names on the lines provided.

In came the animals two by two,
<u>Bumblebees</u>, <u>ants</u>, and <u>caterpillars</u>, too!

Extension Activities

- Learn to sing the popular, traditional song, "Who Built the Ark?" It appears on many tapes, including Raffi's *More Singable Songs.* Create a song chart with the lyrics from the Little Book. Use the "call and response" technique to sing the song. Include the verses children have written on page 8 of their Little Books.
- Reproduce extra copies of page 8 to extend the length of the children's books. Have the children try to include animals from each major group (mammals, birds, reptiles, amphibians, insects). The art can be varied by using animal stickers, rubber stamp art animals, or animals cut from wrapping paper or fabric.
- Attach a long sheet of butcher paper or white shelf paper to the wall. Draw or paint an ark on one end. Invite children to draw or paint pairs of animals walking in line to the ark. When complete, practice skip-counting by twos.

Jacob's Ladder

Cover Idea

Glue a ladder fashioned from flat wooden toothpicks to a dark blue construction paper cover. Add wispy cotton clouds and angel stickers.

Inside Pages

Color each page with crayons, markers, or colored pencils. Draw scenery and Jacob running away on page 3. Draw and color a nighttime scene on page 4. Draw ladders on pages 5, 6, and 7. Draw or add angel stickers to page 6. Add the words of God, *This land is for you,* to page 7. Trace the words with gold glitter glue. Write the words *House of God* on the rock on page 8. Then add texture to the pages. For example, add small gravel and green tissue grass to pages 3 and 4, cotton clouds to pages 5, 6, and 7.

Extension Activities

- Attach a large sheet of butcher paper to the wall. Add the title, *Jacob's Ladder.* Glue strips of gold or brown construction paper to create a ladder on the chart. Add words, phrases, or pictures describing inspiring messages to the rungs of the ladder. Some examples are *Be Kind, Be Helpful, Give to Others, Do Thoughtful Deeds,* etc.
- Referring to the poster above for inspiration, help the children make their own Jacob's Ladder mini-books. Accordion-fold a strip of white construction paper for each child to create the mini book and have him or her add the title *(child's name) Can Climb Jacob's Ladder* to the top section. On each section of the book, the children can write and/or illustrate good works they will do to "climb Jacob's Ladder."

Baby Moses

Cover Idea

Cut a basket shape from tan or brown construction paper. (Or use basket-weave contact paper.) Add details using crayons or markers. Glue small pieces of straw or raffia to the basket. Make a baby Moses from construction paper and attach him to the basket. Add a blanket cut from a fabric scrap to cover the baby.

Inside Pages

Color the pictures using crayons, markers, or colored pencils. Add texture by gluing pieces of raffia and green tissue to pages 2 through 4 and 7. Glue small pieces of blue tissue paper to the water on pages 3 through 5.

Extension Activities

- Help the children make up a tune to go with the text. (Note: "Row, Row, Row Your Boat" works well.) Sing other songs about Moses.
- With the children, create a big book about the major events in the life of Moses. Include Baby Moses, The Burning Bush, The Plagues of Egypt, Crossing the Red Sea, and Moses Receives God's Laws.
- Discuss with the children the people in their lives who take care of them. Let them create their own little books depicting these people. The children could include parents, grandparents, babysitters, doctors, dentists, etc. Help the children add text and tell them to illustrate each page.

Moses and God's Laws

Cover Idea

Cut two "tablets of stone" from gray construction paper for a cover. Add the standard numerals 1–10.

Inside Pages

On page 3, draw or cut out pictures of children from magazines to form a collage. On pages 4 through 7, draw pictures that show how to follow God's laws described on each page. On page 8, draw a self-portrait.

Extension Activities

- Refer to pages 4 through 7 of the Little Book. On a chart, list the eight commandments that have been paraphrased for young children. Leave spaces between each one. Discuss some of the many ways children can follow each of God's laws. Write these under each section of the chart. For example, under, "We love, help, and obey our parents," add things like *I can do my chores without my mom telling me; I can make a card for my dad on his birthday; I will help Mom dust.*
- Children can refer to the completed chart described above and act out little scenes with partners. Other children can guess which of the commandments is being dramatized.
- Let the children create other commandments they think Christians should live by. Make a class big book depicting these.
- Let each child choose the commandment he or she feels is the most important. Have the children write their choice and illustrate it. Combine the pages to create a class book.

David and Goliath

Cover Idea

Cut a cover from black construction paper. Write the title *David and Goliath* in large letters, and draw five stone shapes. Outline the letters and stones with a thin line of white glue. When the glue is dry, use oil pastels or colored chalk to color in the letters and stones. Spray with fixative or hairspray to keep the chalk from smearing.

Inside Pages

Finish drawing the pictures of Goliath and David on pages 2 and 3. Add armor made from aluminum foil scraps to Goliath on page 4. Add fabric scraps to David's clothing on page 5. Glue yarn or a piece of a leather shoestring for the sling and glue five stones on page 7.

Extension Activities

- No one wanted to fight the mean giant except for one brave boy—David! David knew that God would protect him. Have each child add an extra page to his or her Little Book. On the extra page, have each child write a prayer asking God for courage to overcome a fear.

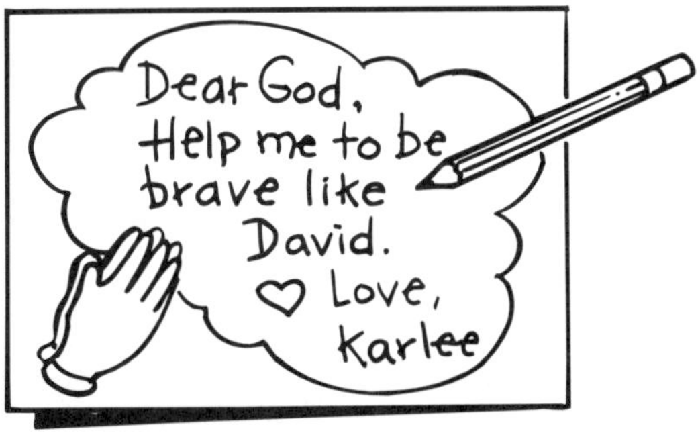

- David overcame an enemy much stronger and bigger than himself because he used his special talent using a sling. Have each child write about one of his or her special talents. Discuss with the children how they can use their talents to make the world a better place.

The Wisdom of Solomon

Cover Idea

Cut a cover from dark blue construction paper. Cut a head, shoulders, and arms shape from brown or tan construction paper and attach it to the cover. Create a portrait of King Solomon by adding details with markers and construction paper scraps. Add yarn for hair, a crown cut from gold metallic wrapping paper, and cloth to King Solomon's robes.

Inside Pages

Decorate the portrait of King Solomon on page 2 similar to the way he was decorated on the cover (see above). Add words to the speech bubbles on pages 4 and 7.

Extension Activities

- Discuss with the children the commonly used expression, "He/she has the wisdom of Solomon." Now is a good time to talk about what people mean when they say this. Discuss times when you and the children acted with the "wisdom of Solomon."
- Explain to the children that we show respect to older people because they have wisdom to share with us. Have them talk with a grandparent or a senior citizen in their family or neighborhood. The children should ask this person to share one good piece of advice with them. Make a class book of wisdom with the advice the children receive.

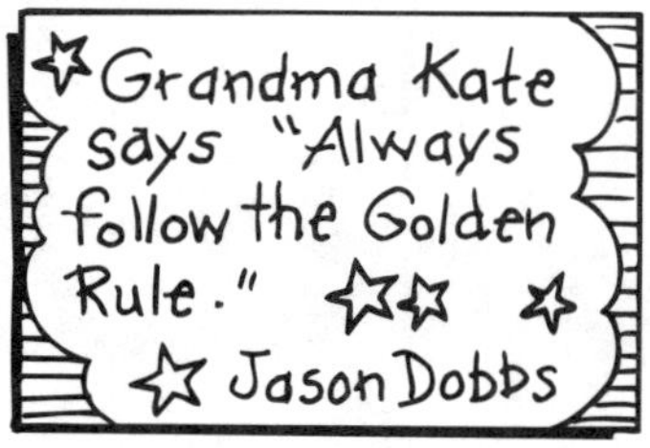

- Discuss other sayings with the children. Read them some verses from the book of Proverbs. Let each child choose a proverb to illustrate (you could provide a list). Assemble the children's pages to create a class book.

Daniel and the Lions

Cover Idea

Illustrate the cover by cutting and pasting construction paper scraps to create Daniel and two lions. Add yellow and orange tissue paper strips to form the mane of each lion.

Inside Pages

In the window on page 2, draw and color the sun, clouds, and birds in the sky. On page 5, write the words *New Law* on the scroll held by the men. In the window on page 6, draw a nighttime scene, including the moon and stars. Draw and color lions on pages 7 and 8.

Extension Activities

- Daniel was faithful to God. This means he was loyal, true, and "stuck by God" even when he had to face punishment. Discuss with the children other people in the Bible who showed faithfulness (Moses, Ruth, Abraham, Noah). Help the children make a class book entitled *Who Is Faithful?* Let each child write a few sentences about a person of his or her choice from the Bible who showed faithfulness (without saying the name) and draw a picture of the person. On the back of the page, have each child write the person's name. When the finished book is read, the children can try to guess who the sentences describe and who the picture depicts before turning over the page.
- Have each child write and illustrate a little book using the sentence starter, *I am faithful to* __________. They can write the sentence starter on several pages and complete each in writing and then illustrate it.

  I am faithful to <u>my friend</u>.

  I am faithful to <u>my parents</u>.

  I am faithful to <u>my brother</u>.

  I am faithful to <u>God</u>.

Esther the Queen

Cover Idea

Decorate a portrait of Esther with a gold crown. Glue gold rickrack and sequins to Esther's gown.

Inside Pages

Finish drawing and coloring the pictures of the king and Esther on page 3. Add gold foil crowns to their heads. Finish Esther's invitation to Haman on page 6. Draw Esther's people on page 8.

Extension Activities

- Rewrite the story as a little play and write lines for the narrator, Mordecai, Esther, the king, Haman, and the soldiers. Choose parts, make simple costumes, and let the children perform the play for another class or for parents.
- Mordecai told Esther, "You became queen so you could save our people!" Ask the children what they would do if they could become king, queen, or president. Help the children make crowns from orange construction paper. On their crowns, have the children write how they would change the world.

- Have each child look in a newspaper or magazine to find a story about someone who helped other people. The children should cut out the article, glue it to a sheet of paper, and write simply what the article is about and how someone helped someone else. Assemble the pages to create a class book.

Jonah and the Great Fish

Cover Idea

Make a fish or whale-shaped cover from construction paper. Use white construction paper to create a spout. Glue it to the top of the back of the fish.

Inside Pages

Draw the big city in the background on page 2. On page 3, draw Jonah running away. Add clouds, rain, and lightning to page 4. Draw the fish on page 6. On page 7, draw Jonah on dry land. Draw the people at Nineveh who are listening to Jonah teach on page 8.

Extension Activities

- Explain to the children that Jonah tried to run away and hide from God. Sometimes people try to run and hide from their problems because facing problems is hard. Have the children write or dictate something that is hard for them or a problem they have. Then have them tell three ways they can solve their problem. The children can ask friends or classmates to help them with ways to solve their problems.

  Problem: I don't like to do my homework. It's hard!

  Solutions: I can work on my homework with a friend.

  I can work on my homework for ten minutes, then play for ten minutes, and so on. I can use a timer.

  I can save a yummy snack to eat after my homework is done.

- Help each child make a paper doll cutout of Jonah from tagboard. They can store their cutouts in a pocket on the cover of their Little Books. The children can use their cutouts as pointers when reading the story or as props when they retell the story of Jonah.

Literature List

Adventure Bible Handbook by Ed Van der Maas and Richard Osborne (Zondervan Publishing House, 1994)

And God Created Squash: How the World Began by Martha W. Hickman (A. Whitman, 1993)

Bible Stories for Children by Geoffrey Horn and Arthur Cavanaugh (Simon & Schuster, 1980)

The Big Bedtime Book of Bible Stories and Prayers by Debbie T. O'Neal (Abingdon Press, 1995)

The Children's Book of Virtues edited by William J. Bennett (Simon & Schuster, 1996)

Creation by Laurie Lazzaro Knowlton (Grace Publications, 1997)

The Early Reader's Big Book of Bible Learning by V. Gilbert Beers (Gold & Honey Books, 1995)

First Bible Story Book by May Hoffman (Dorling Kindersley, 1996)

Gold 'n' Honey Bible by Melody Carlson (Gold & Honey Books, 1997)

Jonah and the Whale by Laurie Lazzaro Knowlton (Grace Publications, 1997)

Joseph's Coat by Laurie Lazzaro Knowlton (Grace Publications, 1997)

Let There Be Light illustrated by Jane Ray (Dutton Children's Books, 1997)

Little Eyes by Kenneth N. Taylor (Omega Publications)

My First Bible retold by Linda Hayward (Random House, 1994)

Noah's Ark by Laurie Lazzaro Knowlton (Grace Publications, 1997)

Noah's Ark retold by Lucy Cousins (Candlewick Press, 1993)

Prayers for Little Hearts by Elena Kucharik (Tyndale, 1996)

Reader's Digest Bible for Children retold by Marie-Helene Delval (Reader's Digest Young Families, 1995)

Tapestries: Stories of Women in the Bible by Ruth Sanderson (Little, Brown, 1998)

The Toddler's Bible Library by V. Gilbert Beers (Victor Books, 1993)

Tomie de Paola's Book of Bible Stories by Tomie de Paola (Putnam Publishing, 1990)

Two by Two by Susan Traugh and Steven Traugh (Grace Publications, 1997)

Drawing Books

Draw Fifty Series by Lee J. Ames (Doubleday)

Ed Emberley's Drawing Book: Make a World by Ed Emberley (Little, Brown, 1972)

Ed Emberley's Drawing Book of Animals by Ed Emberley (Little, Brown, 1994)

Ed Emberley's Drawing Book of Faces by Ed Emberley (Little, Brown, 1992)

Ed Emberley's Great Thumbprint Drawing Book by Ed Emberley (Little, Brown, 1994)

Ed Emberley's Picture Pie: A Book of Circle Art by Ed Emberley (Little, Brown, 1984)

Let's Draw: Bible Heroes by Anita Ganeri (Random, 1994)

Let's Draw Bible Stories by Henrietta Gambill (Standard Publishing, 1994)

Let's Draw Noah's Ark by Henrietta Gambill (Standard Publishing, 1994)

Music

Wee Sing Bible Songs by Pamela Conn Beall and Susan Hagen Nipp (Price, Stern, Sloan)

Wee Sing More Bible Songs by Pamela Conn Beall and Susan Hagen Nipp (Price, Stern, Sloan)

God Made the World

In the beginning God created the heavens and the earth. (Genesis 1:1)

On the first day, God said,
"Let there be light."
God made the day.
God made the night.

God Made the World written by Rozanne Lanczak Williams

On the second day,
God made the sky—
The sky so wide,
The sky so high.

On the third day,
God made the land and seas,
Rivers and mountains,
Flowers and trees.

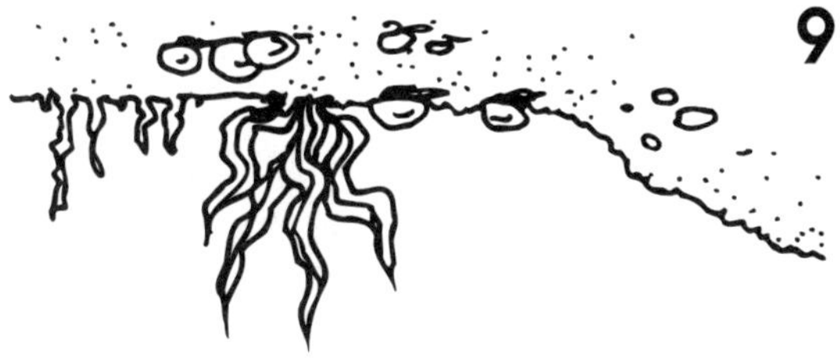

On the fifth day,
God made the fish in the sea,
And birds in the sky—
Birds flying free.

On the fourth day,
God made the sun, the biggest light.
Then God made the moon
And the stars in the night.

On the sixth day,
God made animals, big and small.
Then God made people
To take care of them all.

And God saw that it was good.

On the seventh day,
God took a rest.
This day was holy.
This day was blessed.

God Made the World written by Rozanne Lanczak Williams

Who built the ark? Noah! Noah!
Who built the ark?
Brother Noah built the ark.

"I have set my rainbow in the clouds, and it will be the sign of the covenant between me and the earth." (Genesis 9:13)

Brother Noah built the ark.
He built it out of hickory bark.

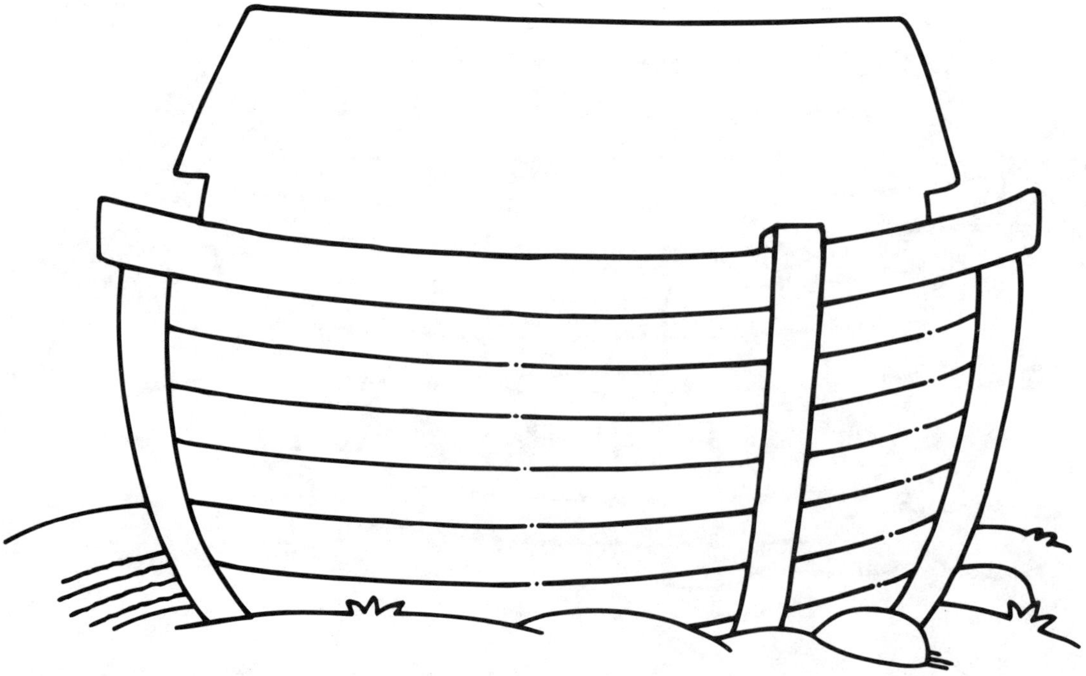

He built it long and wide and tall,
With plenty of room for the large and small.

Who Built the Ark? Traditional song adapted by Rozanne Lanczak Williams

In came the animals two by two,
Hippopotamus and kangaroo.

In came the animals two by two,
The sheep went, "Ba-a-a!"
And the cows went, "Moo!"

In came the animals two by two,
"Quack! Quack!," "Oink!,"
And "Cock-a-doodle-do!"

In came the animals two by two,

 ____________, ____________, and ____________, too!

Who Built the Ark? Traditional song adapted by Rozanne Lanczak Williams

He had a dream in which he saw a stairway . . .
reaching to heaven . . . (Genesis 28:12)

Jacob and Esau were brothers.
They had a terrible fight.

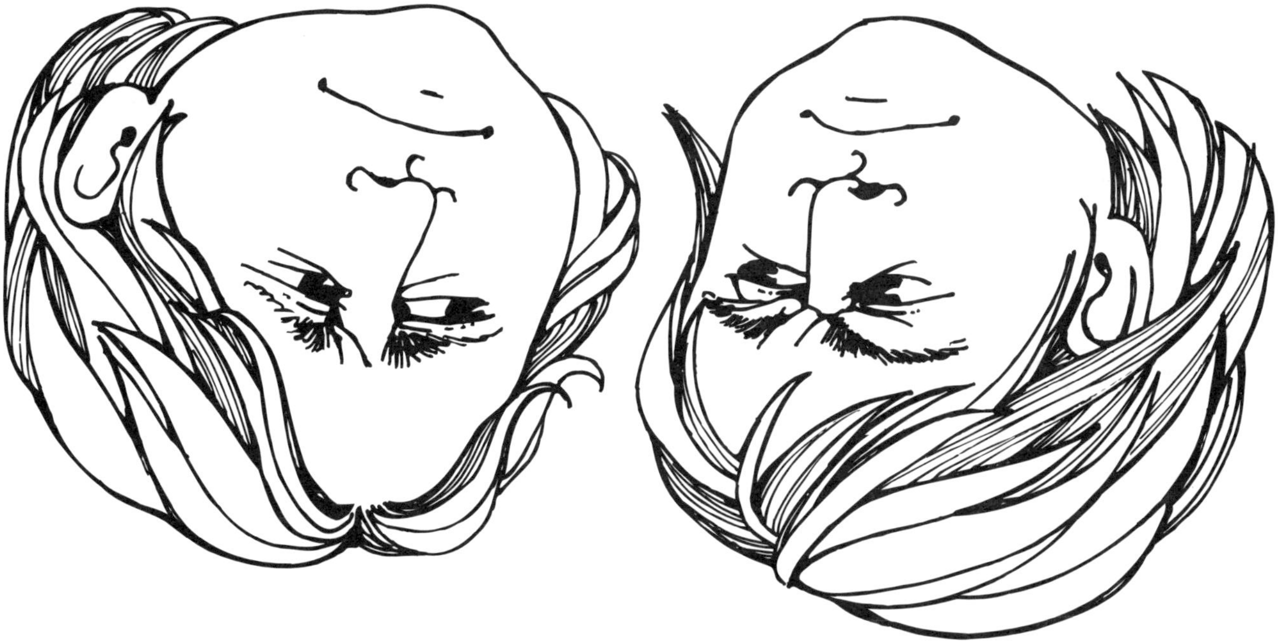

Jacob ran away from Esau.

Jacob stopped to sleep.
He used a rock for a pillow.

Jacob's Ladder retold by Rozanne Lanczak Williams

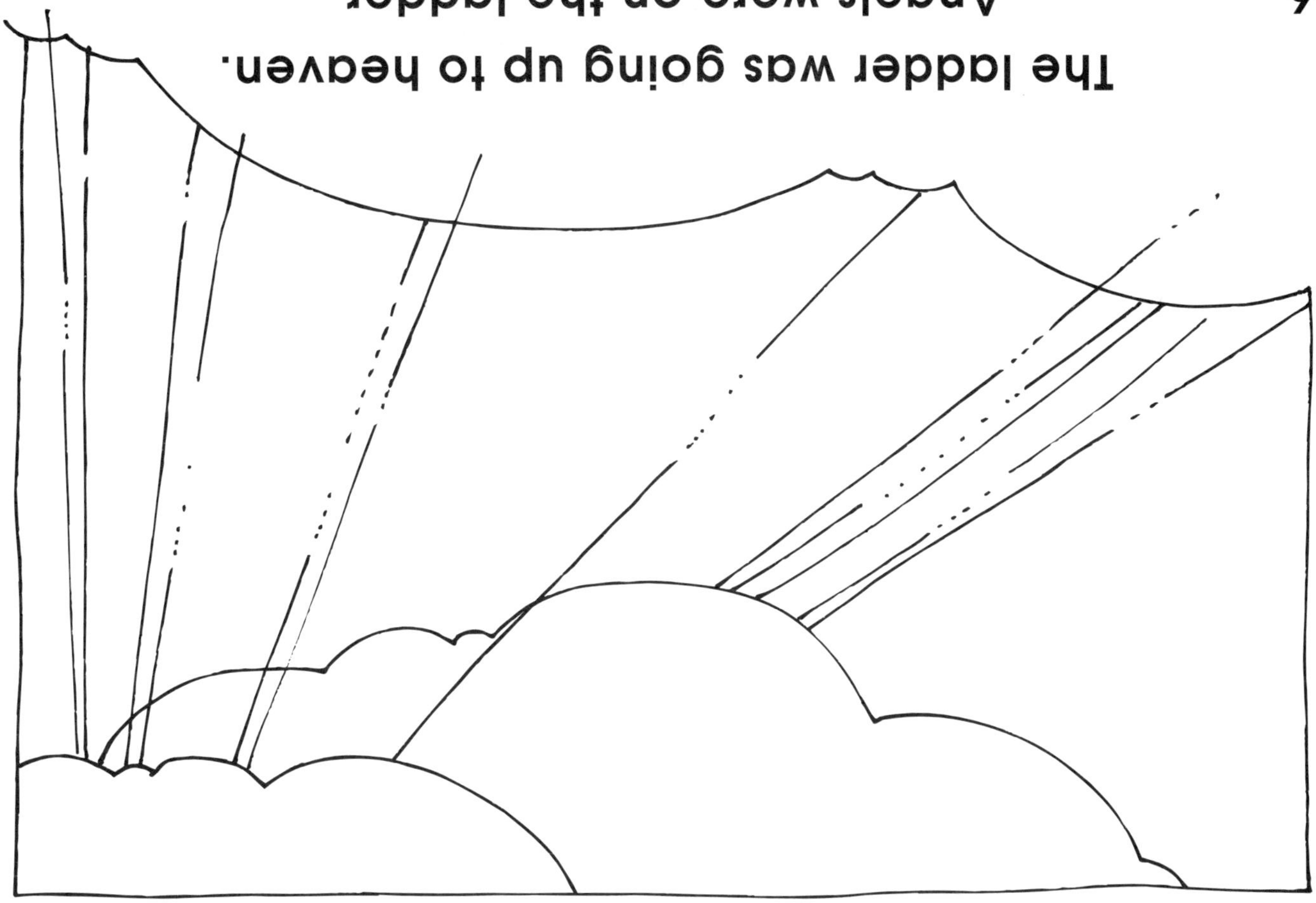

The ladder was going up to heaven.
Angels were on the ladder.

That night, Jacob had a dream.
He dreamed he saw a ladder.

God said to Jacob, "This land is for you.
It is for you and your family forever and ever."

When Jacob woke up, he said,
"This is a holy place.
I will call this place Bethel.
This is the house of God."

Jacob's Ladder retold by Rozanne Lanczak Williams

Hide, hide, hide baby Moses.
Who will hide you away?

Baby Moses written by Rozanne Lanczak Williams

Baby Moses

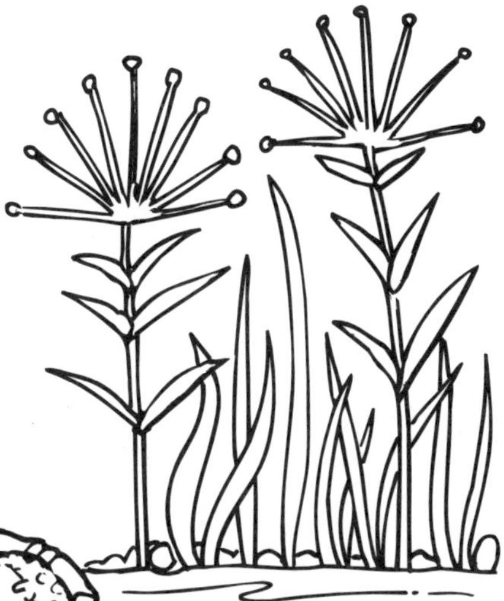

. . . She named him Moses, saying, "I drew him out of the water." **(Exodus 2:10)**

The reeds and rushes by the river's edge
Will hide baby Moses away.

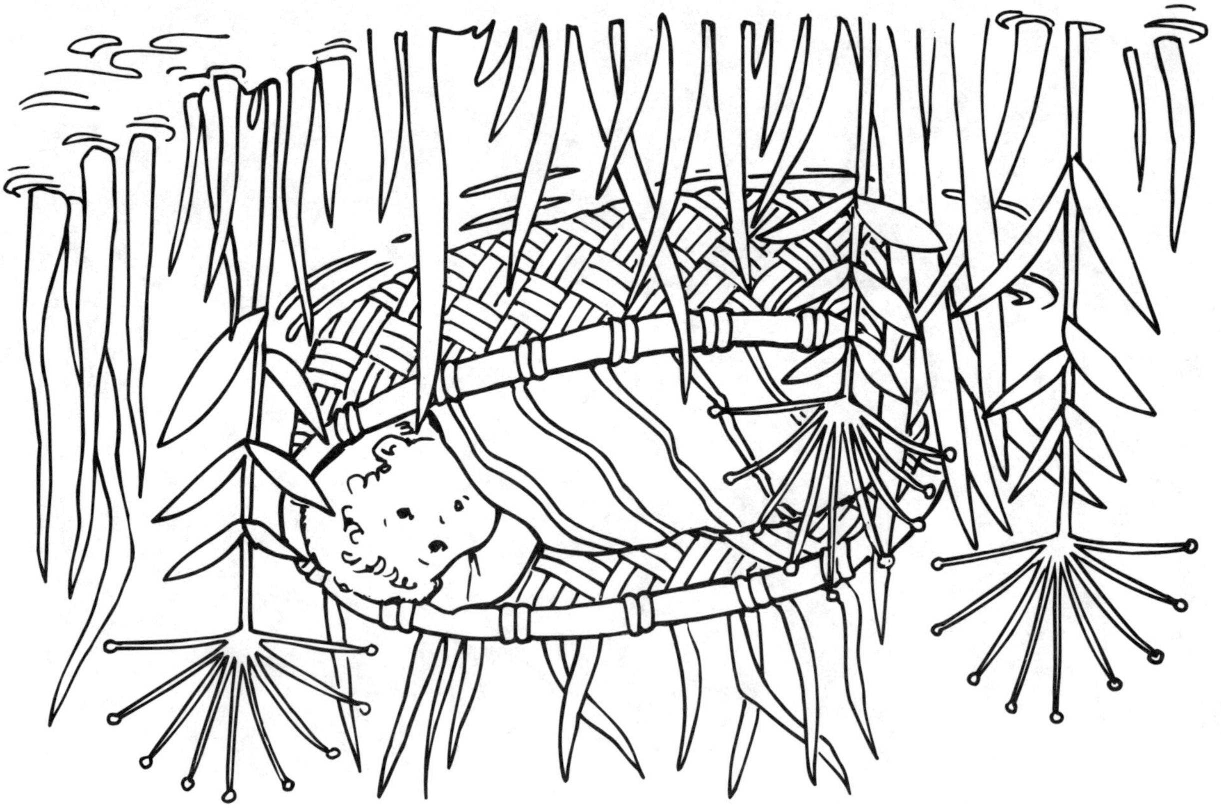

Sleep, sleep, sleep baby Moses.
Who will rock you to sleep?

Baby Moses written by Rozanne Lanczak Williams

Hush! Hush! Hush baby Moses.
Who will dry your tears?

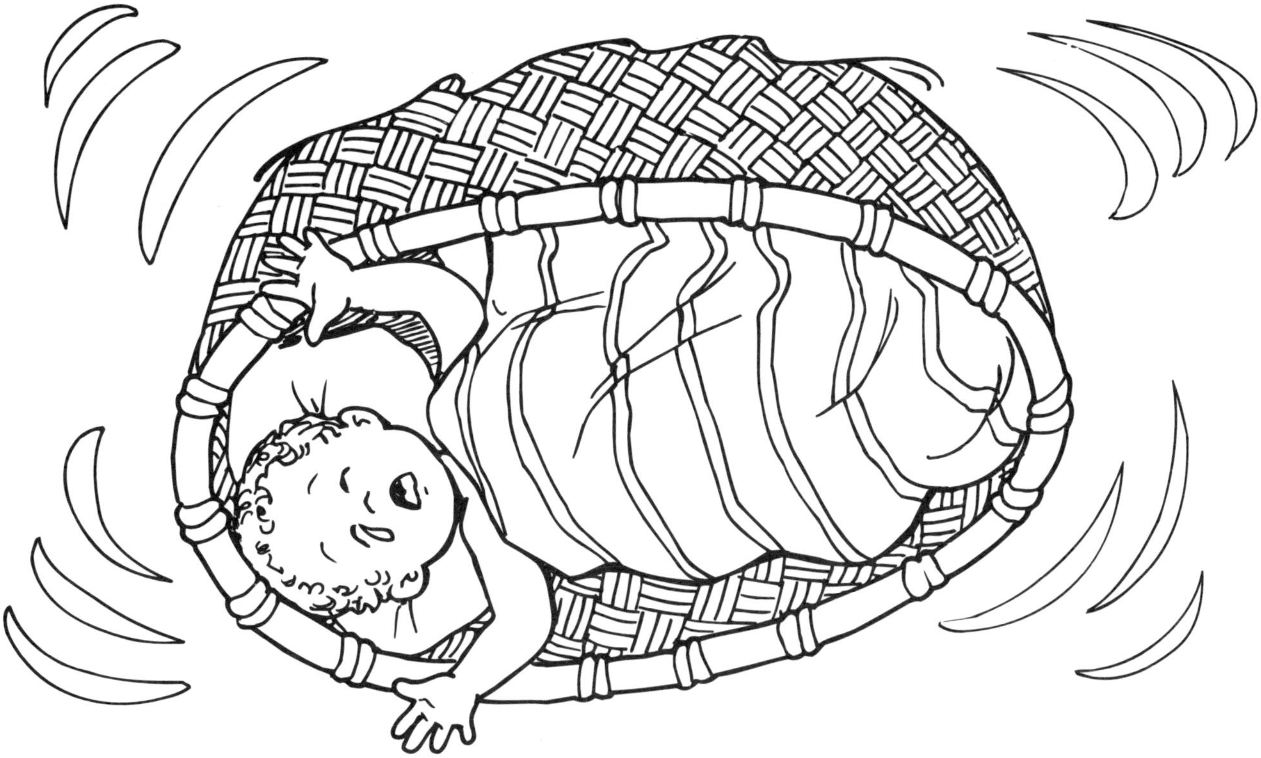

The gentle waters of the Nile
Will rock baby Moses to sleep.

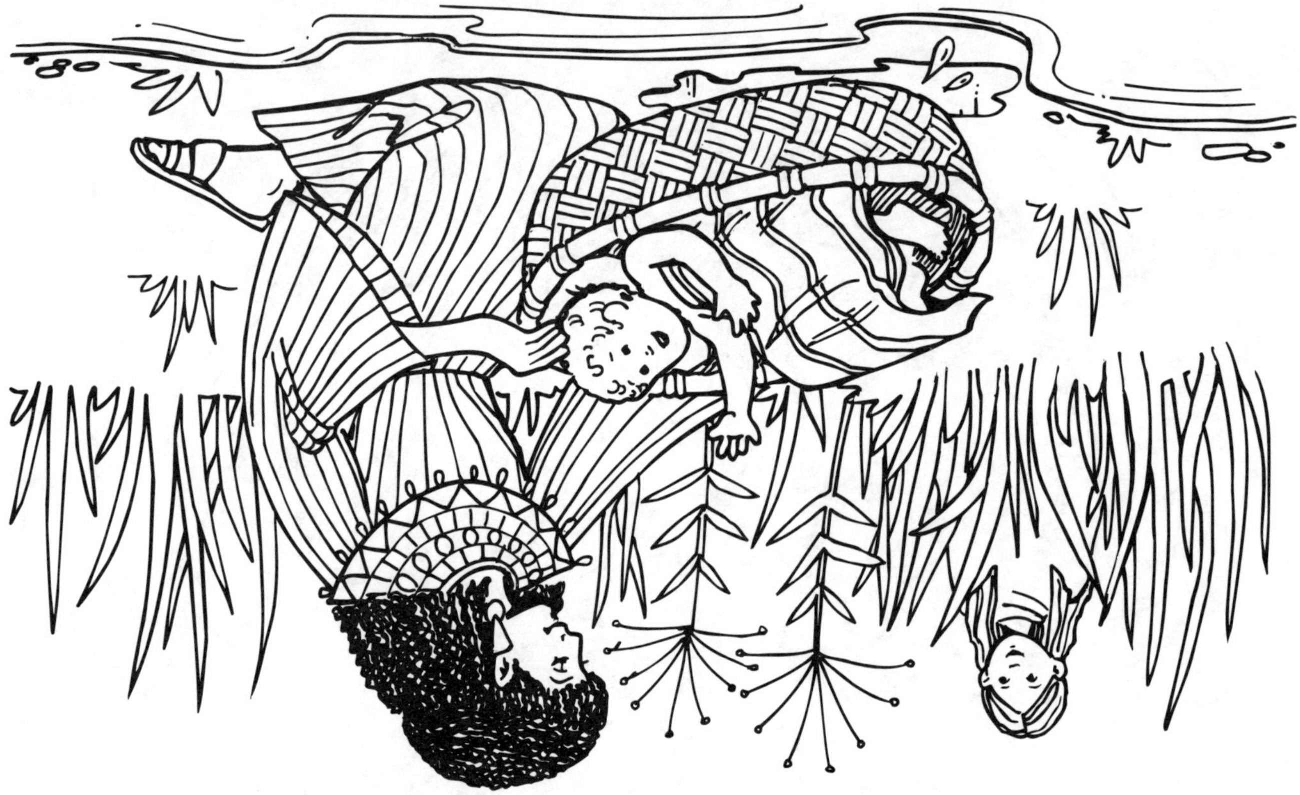

The loving daughter of the king
Will save you and hold you near.

Grow, grow, grow baby Moses.
Who will help you along?
Your very own mother will care for you
And help you grow big and strong.

Baby Moses written by Rozanne Lanczak Williams

Moses

and God's Laws

The Lord descended to the top of Mount Sinai and called Moses to the top of the mountain.

(Exodus 19:20)

Moses climbed the mountain.
He prayed there all alone.
God gave him the Ten Commandments.
Ten laws were carved in stone.

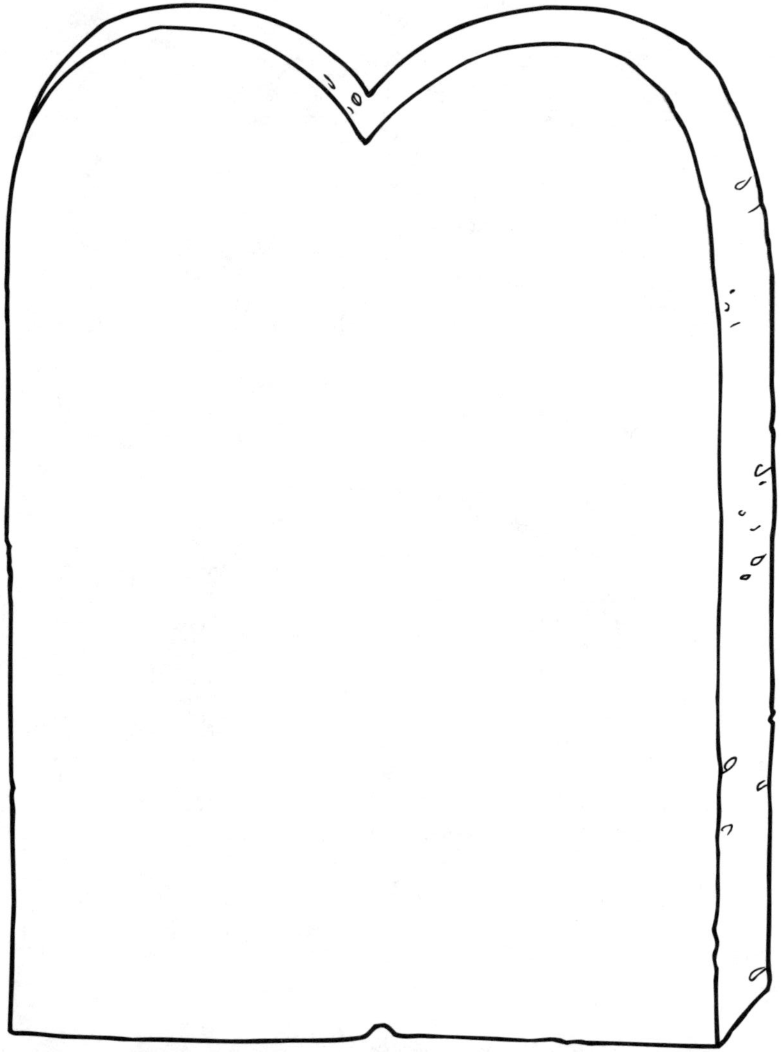

We are little children.
We follow God's laws, too.
We learn from the Ten
Commandments.
Here's what we can do.

Moses and God's Laws retold by Rozanne Lanczak Williams

We believe in God. We love God.

We use God's name with love.

We pray with our family
in church on Sunday.

We love, help, and
obey our parents.

We are kind and
helpful to others.

We tell the truth.

We take care of other
people's things.

We love our neighbors.
We are happy with
what we have.

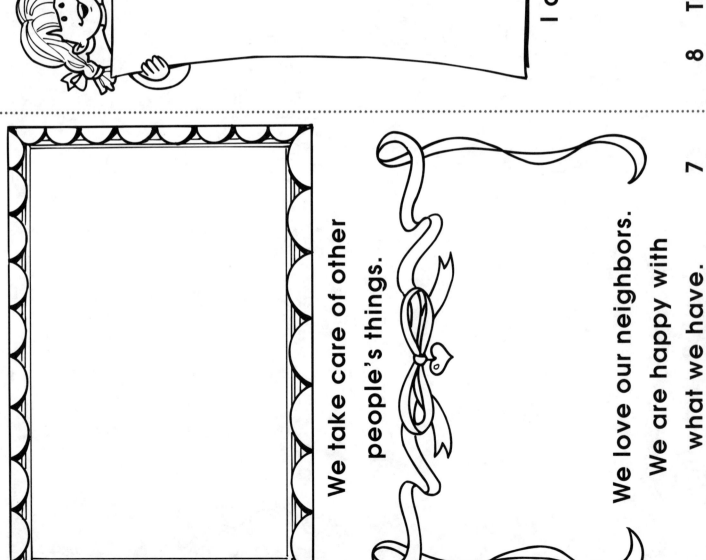

I am one of God's children.
I follow God's laws, too.
I learn from the Ten
Commandments.
There's so much I can do!

David and Goliath

. . . "You come against me with sword and spear . . . but I come against you in the name of the Lord Almighty . . ."

(1 Samuel 17:45)

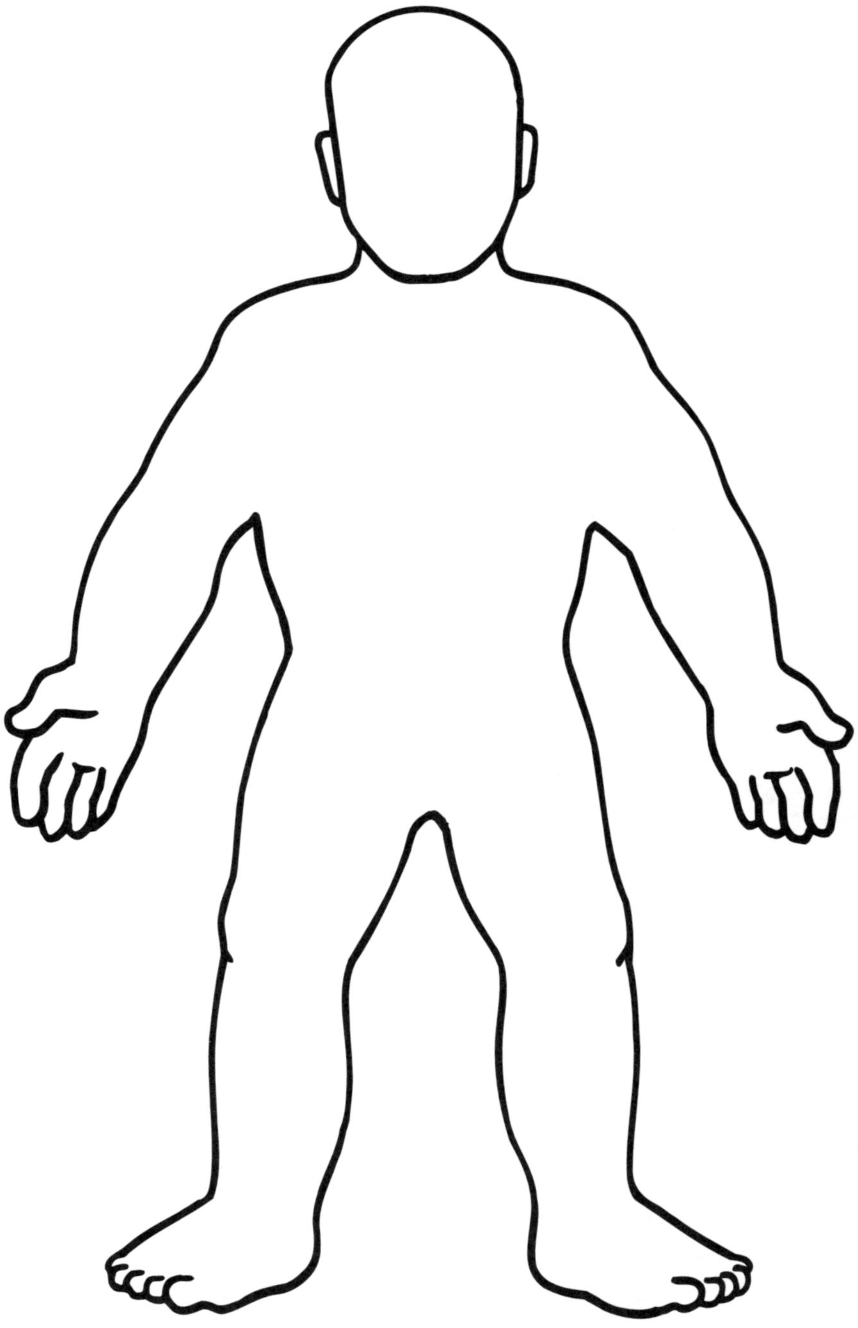

Goliath is a fierce giant.

I am a small boy.
But I come in the
name of God.

Goliath has armor
to protect him.

I have no armor.
But I come in the
name of God.

Goliath carries a sword
and spear.

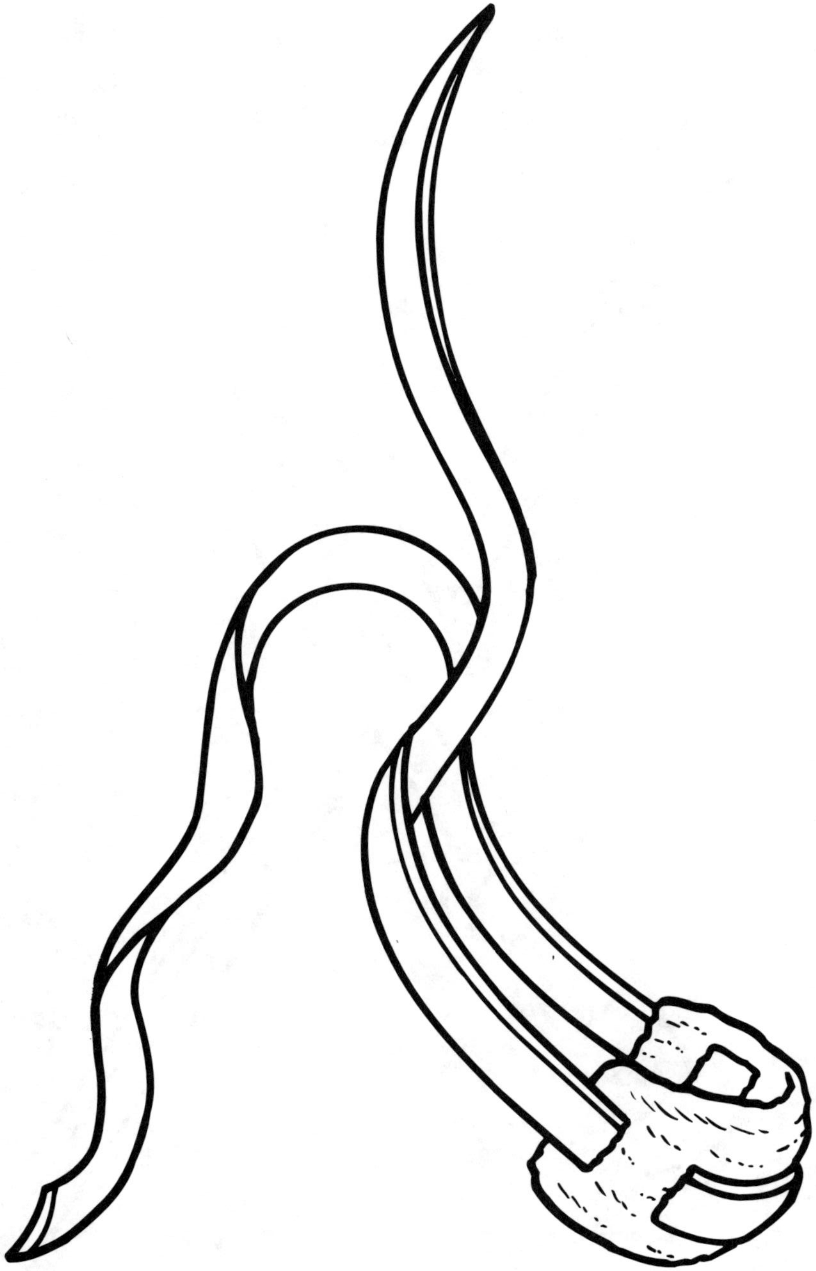

I carry only a sling
and five stones.

I come in the name of God.
And God protects me
from danger.

The Wisdom of Solomon retold by Rozanne Lanczak Williams

The Wisdom of Solomon

Then the king said, "Bring me a sword . . .
Cut the living child in two . . ."
(1 Kings 3:24–25)

Solomon was a wise king.
Solomon was a good king.

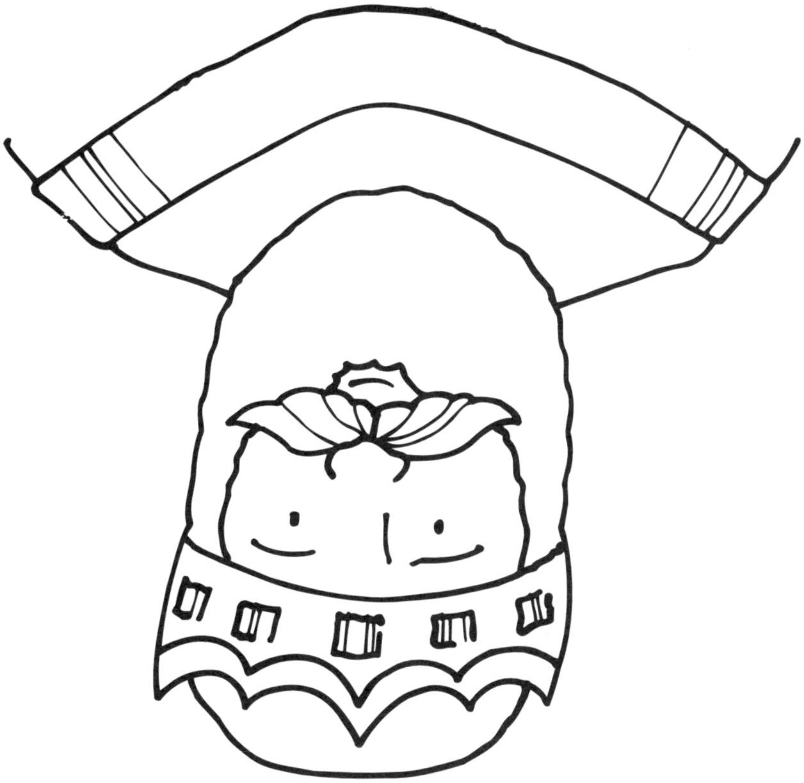

One day, two women came to King Solomon. They had a baby with them.

 One woman said, "This is my baby!"

The Wisdom of Solomon retold by Rozanne Lanczak Williams

The other woman said,
"No, no! This is *my* baby!
She took my baby while I was sleeping."

King Solomon said,
"Bring me my sword.
I will give each woman half."

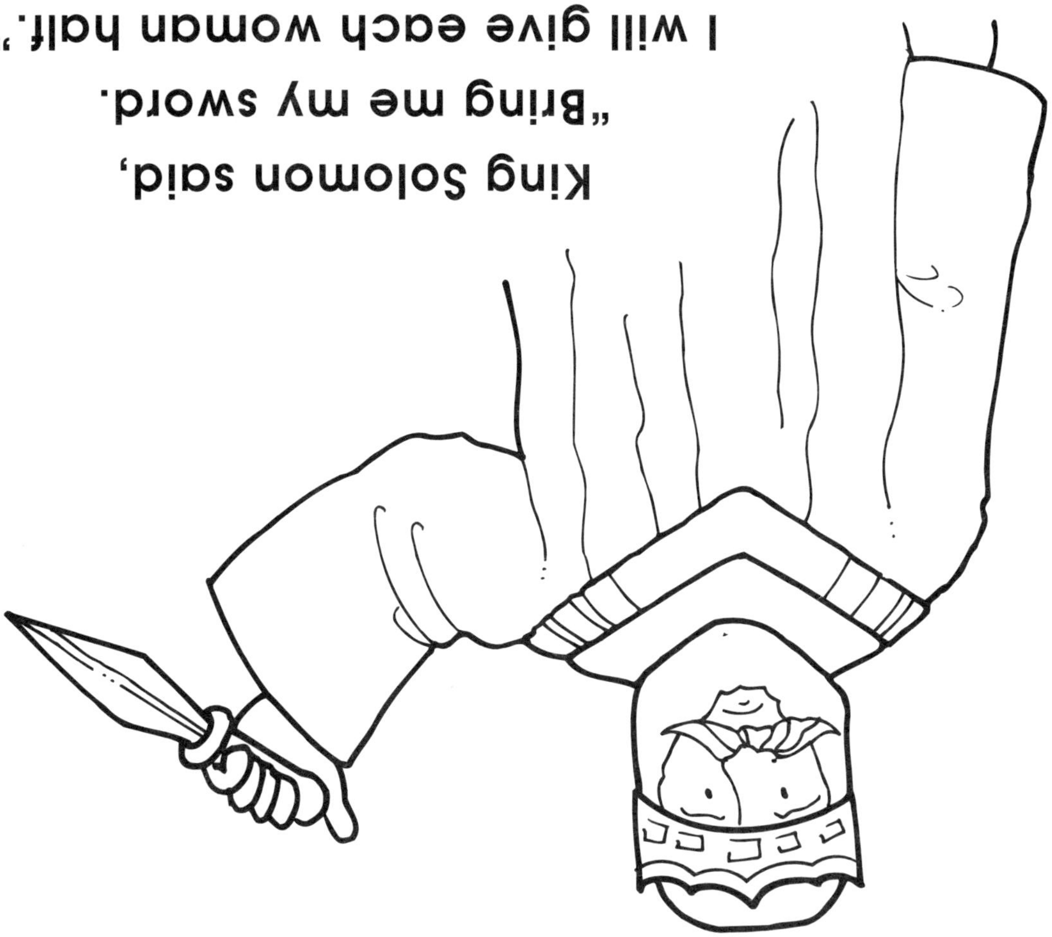

"Yes," said one woman.
The other woman cried,
"No, no! Do not kill my baby!
Let her have the baby."

King Solomon knew who the real mother was.
He gave the baby to the crying woman.

Daniel and the Lions

. . . And when Daniel was lifted from the den, no wound was found on him, because he had trusted in his God. (Daniel 6:23)

Daniel was a good and wise man.
Daniel prayed to God three times a day.

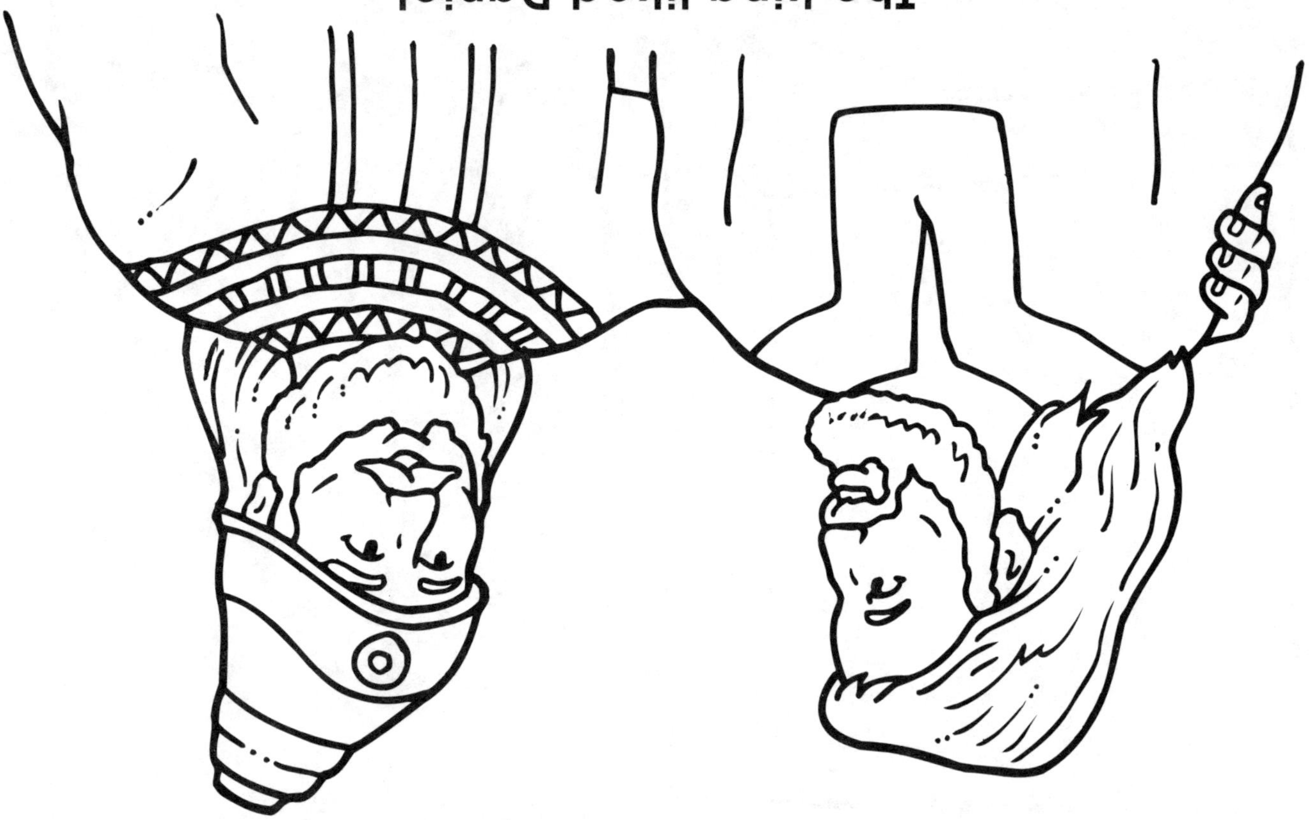

The king liked Daniel.
The king gave Daniel the best job.

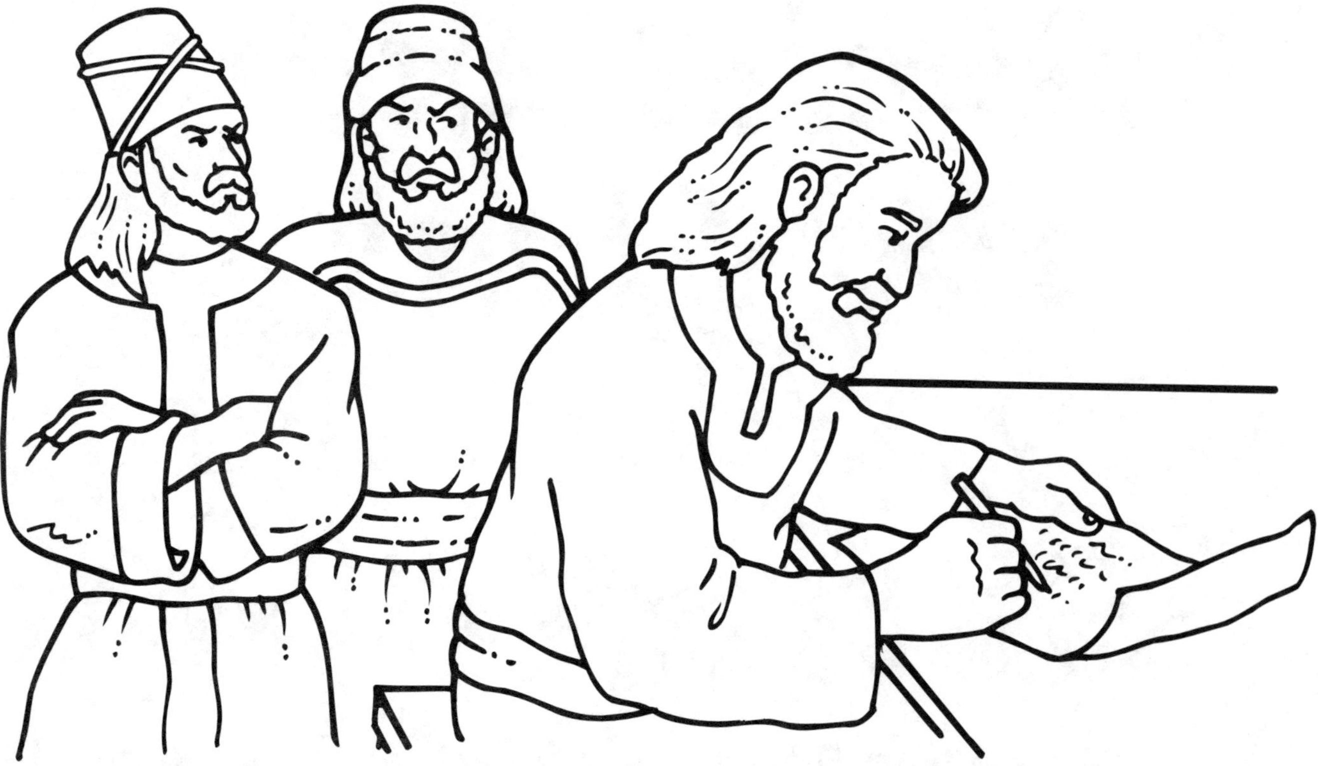

Some men did not like Daniel
because he had the best job.

Daniel and the Lions retold by Rozanne Lanczak Williams

Daniel prayed to God three times a day.

But Daniel prayed only to God.

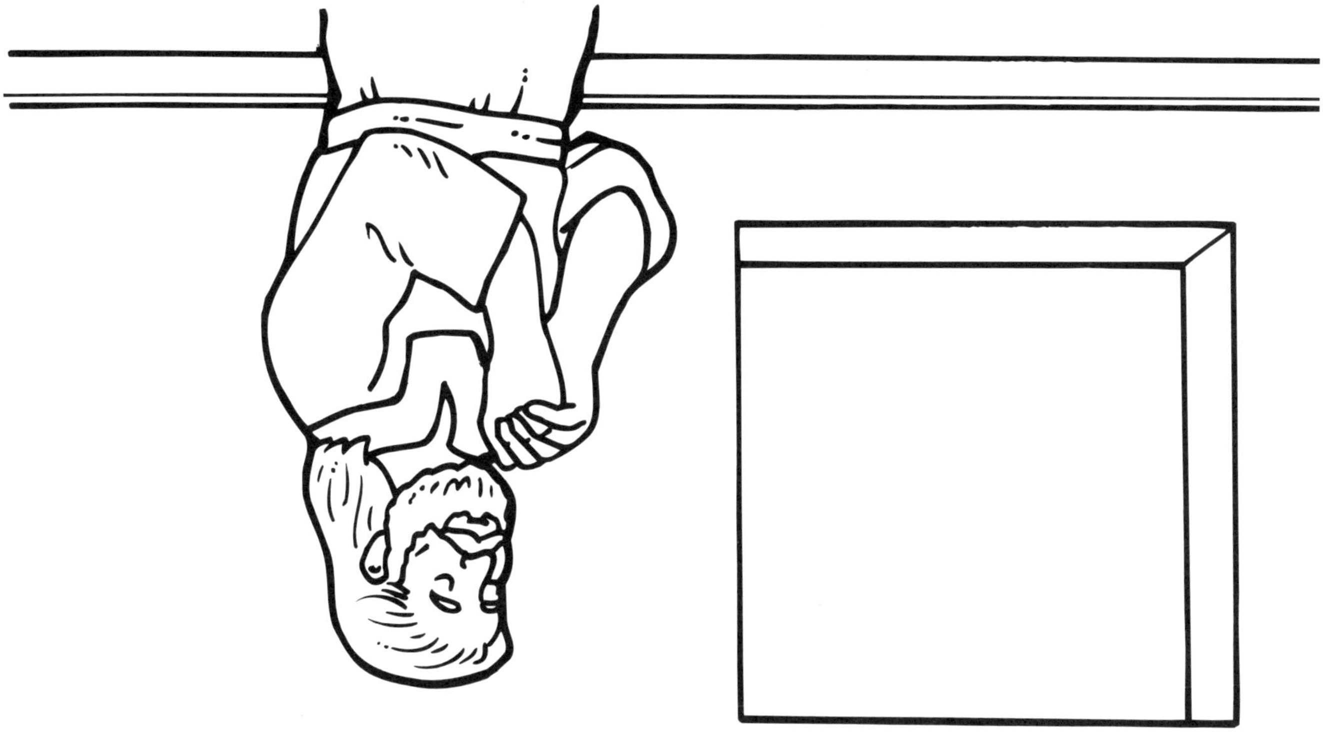

The men asked the king to make a law:

“Pray only to the king!”

Daniel did not pray to the king.
So Daniel was put in the lions' den.
Daniel prayed all night.

The lions did not eat Daniel!
"Your God is the only God," said the king.

Daniel and the Lions retold by Rozanne Lanczak Williams

Esther the Queen

"For how can I bear to see disaster fall on my people? . . ." (Esther 8:6)

Esther was a smart and beautiful woman. 1

The king of Persia was looking for a new queen.

Mordecai, Esther's cousin, took her to the king. 2

Esther the Queen retold by Rozanne Lanczak Williams

The king liked Esther.

He chose her to be the queen.

An evil man, Haman, hated Mordecai.

He wanted to kill Mordecai.

He wanted to kill all of Esther's people.

Esther the Queen retold by Rozanne Lanczak Williams

Mordecai heard about the evil plan.

He went to Esther.

Esther invited Haman to dinner.

While they ate, she told

the king about the evil plan.

The king was angry. He punished Haman.

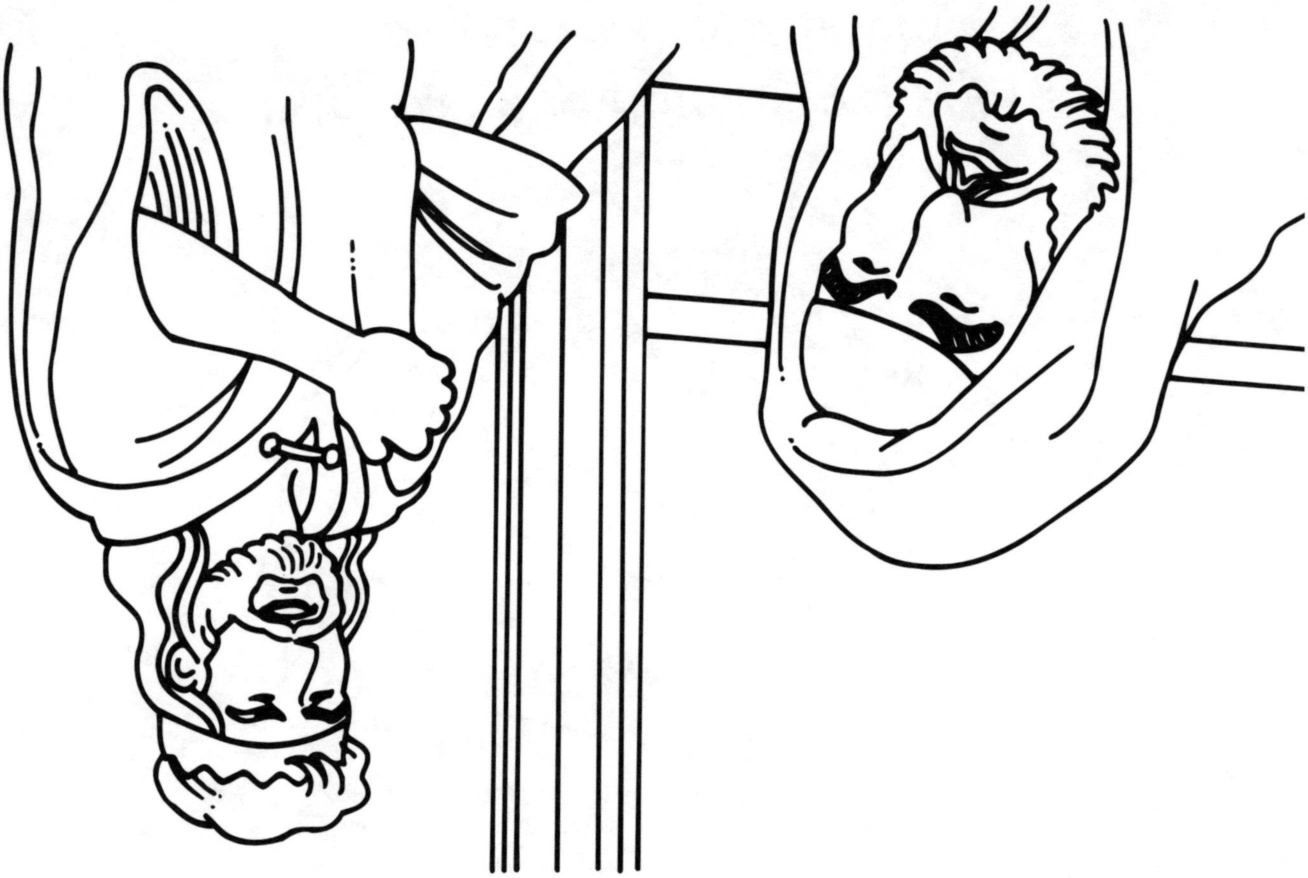

Esther was a great queen.
Esther saved her people!

Esther the Queen retold by Rozanne Lanczak Williams

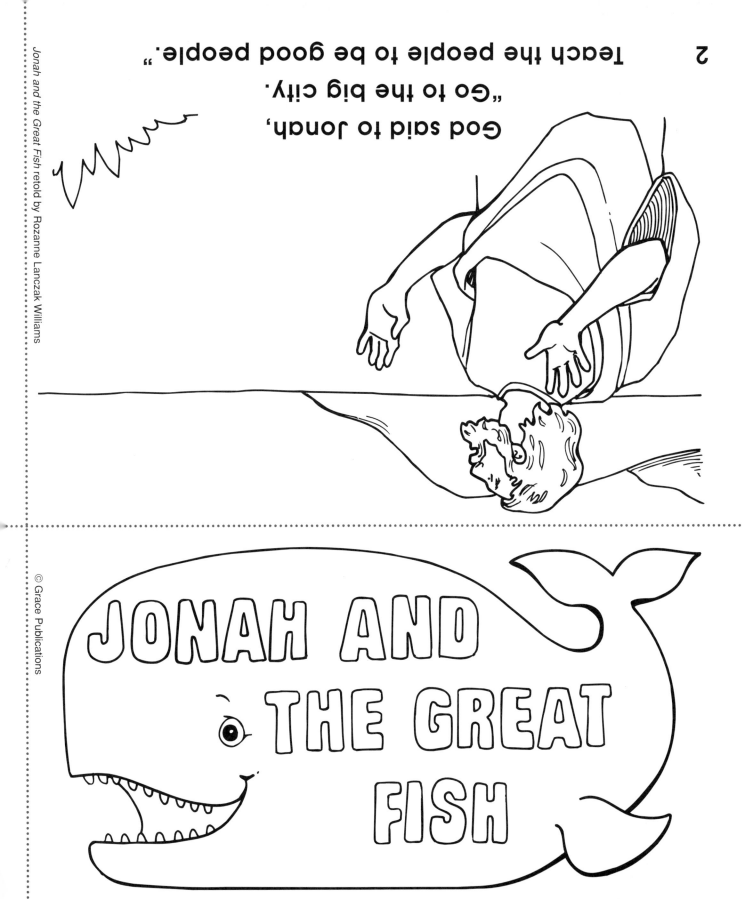

But the Lord provided a great fish to swallow Jonah, and Jonah was inside the fish three days and three nights. **(Jonah 1:17)**

God said to Jonah,
"Go to the big city.
Teach the people to be good people."

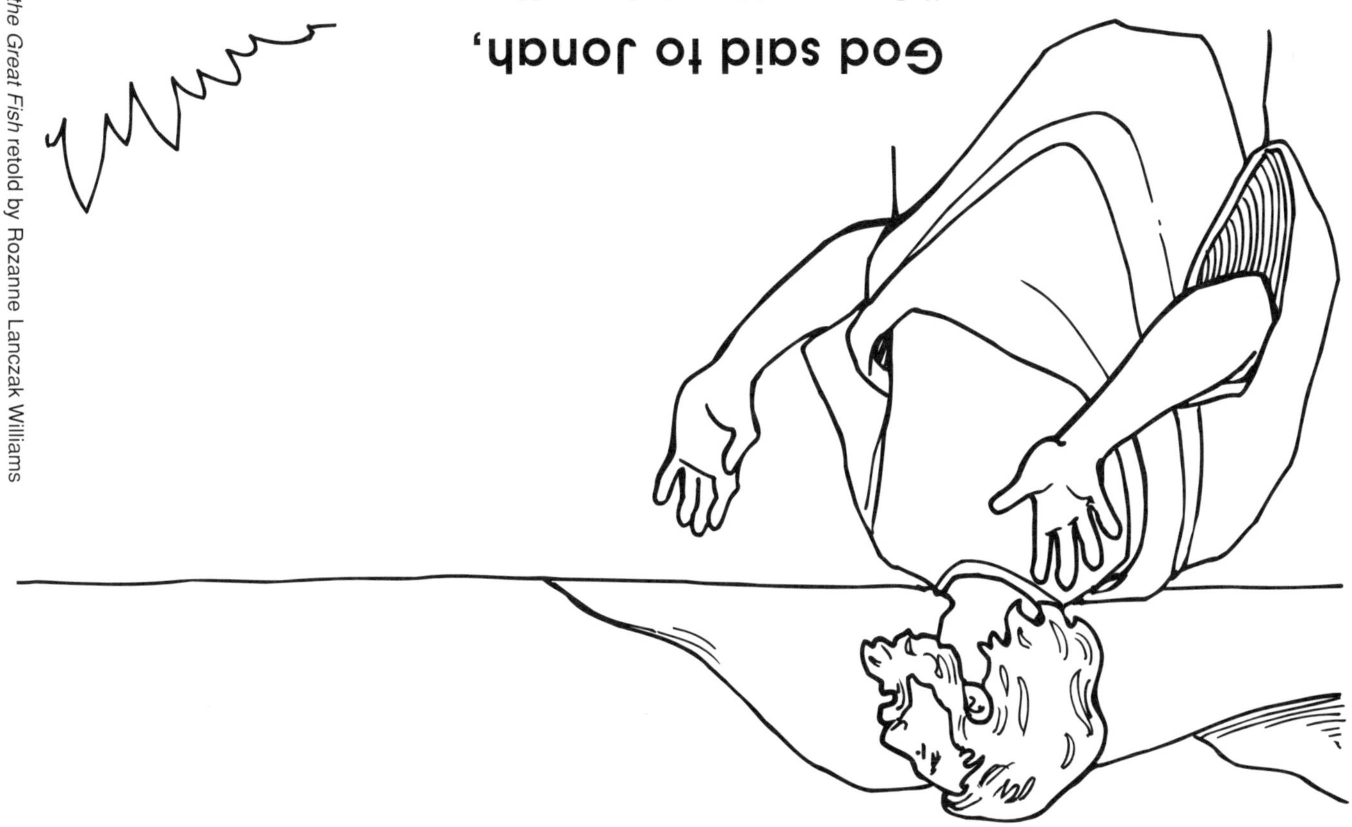

Jonah and the Great Fish retold by Rozanne Lanczak Williams

Jonah did not want to go to the city.
He ran away.

Jonah got on a ship.
Jonah hid from God.
But God saw Jonah.
God sent a big storm.

Jonah and the Great Fish retold by Rozanne Lanczak Williams

A big fish swallowed Jonah.

Jonah was inside the fish for three days.

Jonah prayed to God.

The ship was sinking. Jonah said, "This is my fault."

The others on the ship threw Jonah into the water.

The storm stopped.

God heard Jonah's prayer.
The fish took Jonah to dry land.

Jonah said, "I will listen to God."
Jonah went to the big city.
He helped the people to be good.